Everything you need to know about
SHARKS
AND OTHER CREATURES OF THE DEEP

PREVIOUSLY PUBLISHED AS SHARKS AND OTHER CREATURES OF THE DEEP

LONDON, NEW YORK, MUNICH,
MELBOURNE, and DELHI

Editors Penny Smith, Ann Baggaley, Elinor
Greenwood, Elizabeth Haldane, Wendy
Horobin, Cécile Landau, Deborah Lock, Carrie
Love, Lorrie Mack, Sue Malyan, Caroline
Stamps, Steve White-Thomson, Lee Wilson
Designers Gemma Fletcher, Simon Balley,
Jess Bentall, Emma Forge, Tom Forge, Hedi
Gutt, Karen Hood, Sonia Moore, Clémence de
Moulliens, Claire Patane, Sophie Pelham, Joanna
Pocock, Laura Roberts, Rachael Smith, Sadie
Thomas, Vicky Wharton

Consultant Trevor Day
Picture Research Frances Vargo
Publishing Manager Bridget Giles
Art Director Rachael Foster
Category Publisher Mary Ling
Creative Director Jane Bull

THIS EDITION
Managing Editor Julie Ferris
Managing Art Editor Owen Peyton Jones
US Editor Margaret Parrish
Jacket Designer Laura Brim
Production Controller Erika Pepe
Production Editor Luca Frassinetti
Publisher Sarah Larter
Associate Publishing Director Liz Wheeler
Art Director Phil Ormerod
Publishing Director Jonathan Metcalf

DK Delhi
Managing Editor Alka Thakur
Editors Anita Kakar, Ritu Mishra
Consultant Art Director Shefali Upadhyay
Designers Sudakshina Basu, Arijit Ganguly,
Mahua Mandal, Ivy Roy
Production Manager Pankaj Sharma
DTP Manager Balwant Singh
DTP Designers Harish Aggarwal,
Shanker Prasad

Previously published in 2008 as
Sharks and Other Creatures of the Deep
This abridged edition published in
the United States in 2012 by DK Publishing, Inc.
345 Hudson Street, New York, New York 10014

13 14 15 16 10 9 8 7 6 5 4 3
006—186591—June/12

Discover more at **www.dk.com**

CONTENTS

4   Water

6   Ideal homes

8   Who's who of the
    watery world

10 What is a fish?

12 This is not a fish… it's
    a mammal

14 Shark facts and stats

16 Shark's skin makes waves

18 Toothless wonders

20 Heart of darkness

22 Now you see me…

24 Who's not the fairest
    of them all?

26 Ocean homes

28 Fueling the nation

30 What's inside a shell?

32 What's inside a fish?

34 A long way home

36 What am I?

38 The shocking truth

40 Friend or food?

42 Cleaning stations

44 Glow-in-the-dark

46 Surviving the deep

48 Who's the daddy?

50 Danger in the water!

52 Things that sting

54 Who's a pretty boy?

56 Prickly character

58 Coming up for air

60 Saved by slime

62 Pulling the trigger!

64 Synchronized swimming

66 Apple of his eye

68 Animals at risk

70 Talking fish

72 Changing colors

74 Record breakers

76 High seas drifters

78 Glossary and index

Water may be the most common compound in the universe. The Earth has **369 million trillion gallons** of the stuff, which works out to about **57 billion gallons** for every **person** alive. If you filled a balloon with all the Earth's water, it would be about a third the diameter of the Moon. Some comes from **COMETS**, which have **sprinkled** their water into the Earth's atmosphere over **billions** of years.

Scientists think that several million

Some of our water comes from *"wet rocks"* beneath the Earth's surface, whose moisture is released by volcanoes as *steam*. Luckily for us, the Earth is just the right distance from the Sun for water to be liquid. If we were any nearer or farther, the oceans would **boil** or **freeze**, and **life** couldn't exist. Life on Earth probably began in the **OCEANS**, and all living organisms are based on saltwater. Human beings are mostly *water*, with a few other things thrown in. We are directly descended from **FISH**, which first walked on land more than **355** million years ago.

Water baby
A human being is an aquatic animal for the first nine months of its life, when it lives in a pool of saltwater inside its mother's womb.

species of animal and plant live in the Earth's water.

Ideal homes: sea views guaranteed →

Open oceans

The open oceans are the largest habitat on the planet. The upper zones of the open sea, far from land, teem with fish and other marine life of all kinds. Meanwhile, down in the depths, strange creatures roam in the darkness, waiting for dinner to come their way.

What lives in the open ocean?

- Herrings: predatory fish and people love to eat these.
- Sardines: this is where they hang out before being put in a can.
- Tuna: eat the herrings and sardines—then they get eaten by sharks and people.
- Marlin: these big fish are a popular gamefish, hunted by humans.
- Dolphins: hunt in pods in the open ocean.
- Sharks: live in every ocean of the world.
- Whales: where else could animals this big live?

Many types of fish spend their entire lives, day and night, swimming. They can drift with the currents for a rest. The water supports their bodies, so they don't use much energy and don't get tired.

Kelp forests

These are like tropical jungles on land, but instead of trees, giant seaweeds grow up toward the light. Fish find a safe haven among the fronds. Marine otters wrap themselves in kelp then nap without drifting away. It's a distinctly lush environment, although chilly.

What lives in the kelp forest?

- Sea urchins: the baddies of the forest, they graze on the kelp, cutting it loose so it dies.
- Turban snails: prettier versions of the snails in your yard, but they still make holes in underwater plants.
- Kelp crabs: these gardeners prune out the old kelp fronds.
- Bat star: eats up the debris on the seafloor.
- Blue rockfish: live in swarms among the kelp, gobbling up jellyfish and plankton.
- Sea otters: these good guys snack on sea urchins while looking cool and laid-back.

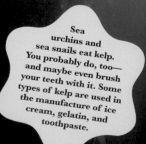

Sea urchins and sea snails eat kelp. You probably do, too—and maybe even brush your teeth with it. Some types of kelp are used in the manufacture of ice cream, gelatin, and toothpaste.

Sea creatures set up home in all kinds of underwater places. Here are four of their favorite aquatic habitats.

Cold polar seas

At the top and bottom of the world are the icy waters of the Arctic and Southern oceans. Here, sea ice provides platforms for passing penguins or polar bears. Amazingly, these cold waters are full of life, and in recent years scientists have discovered hundreds of new animals.

What lives in cold polar seas?

• Krill: these tiny crustaceans are vacuumed up in bucketloads by whales, seals, and fish.
• Polar bears: can swim across open water to find food.
• Giant sea spiders: these eight-legged creatures grow to the size of dinner plates.
• Penguins: spend as much time in the water as on the ice. They "fly" underwater.
• Sea cucumbers: these squishy creatures love the cold, dark seabed.
• Walruses: use their tusks to haul themselves on to the ice.

Thick fur and blubber keep a polar bear warm. But most polar fish have a type of antifreeze in their blood that stops them from turning into floating ice pops.

Coral reefs

The colorful coral reefs are full of cracks and crevices where fish can hide. Corals come in all shapes and sizes. Some look like trees, others like lettuces, dinner plates, or fans. There are even round, crinkly corals that look like a human brain.

What lives on a coral reef?

• Sharks: patrol the reef, looking for their next meal.
• Sea anemones: these pretty sea "flowers" spread out long tentacles to trap prey.
• Starfish: some of them gobble up the coral and damage the reef.
• Clownfish: these movie-star fish take shelter among stinging anemones.
• Fan worms: with their stony tubes, they are often mistaken for coral.
• Octopuses: these soft-bodied creatures hide in gaps in the reef.

Large coral reefs can take centuries to develop. Some of the oldest coral reefs are between 5,000 and 10,000 years old. Australia's Great Barrier Reef is the biggest reef system in the world.

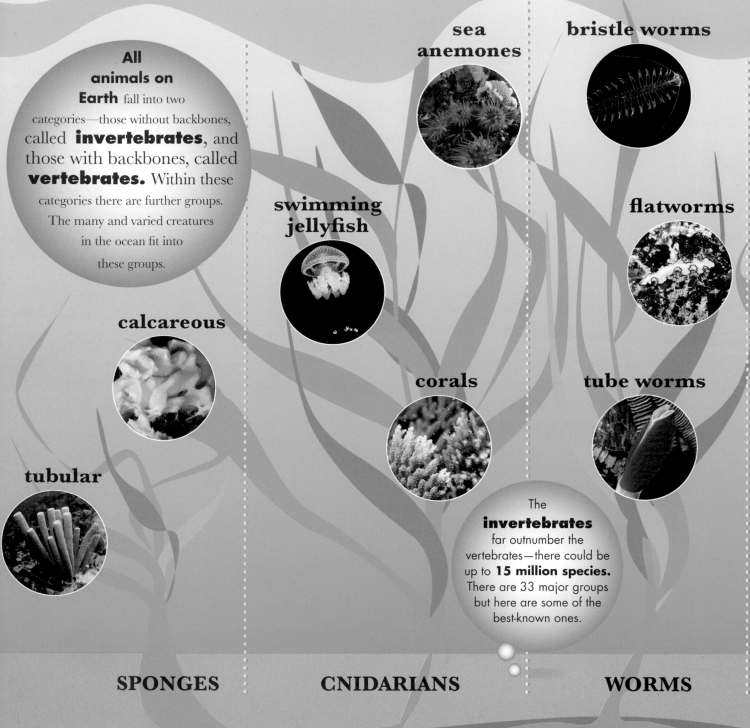

All animals on Earth fall into two categories—those without backbones, called **invertebrates**, and those with backbones, called **vertebrates.** Within these categories there are further groups. The many and varied creatures in the ocean fit into these groups.

sea anemones

bristle worms

swimming jellyfish

flatworms

calcareous

corals

tube worms

tubular

The **invertebrates** far outnumber the vertebrates—there could be up to **15 million species.** There are 33 major groups but here are some of the best-known ones.

SPONGES   **CNIDARIANS**   **WORMS**

Invertebrates...

world

Mammals such as whales, dolphins, seals, and walruses

clams, oysters, and scallops

brittle stars

Reptiles such as turtles

marine insects

sea slugs and snails

sea cucumbers

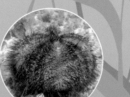

Fish such as **sharks, rays, herring,** and **salmon**

shrimp, crabs, and lobsters

sea urchins

octopuses, squid, and cuttlefish

starfish

Some **vertebrates** are the **biggest** creatures in the ocean.

sea spiders

ARTHROPODS   **MOLLUSKS**   **ECHINODERMS**   **CHORDATES**

and more **Invertebrates...**   **Vertebrates**

What is a fish?

The earliest fish appeared on Earth more than **460 million years ago**. They were the first-ever animals with backbones. Compared to fish, humans are a recent arrival! There are some **25,000 different types, or species, of fish**. Streamlined, slithery, and scaly, they are tailor-made for a watery lifestyle.

Checklist for a

FISH

- **Gills** The fishy equivalent of lungs. They are thin sheets of tissue, full of blood vessels, that extract oxygen from the water.
- **Scales** A fish's wetsuit. These small plates, made of very thin bone, help to waterproof the fish's body.
- **Fins** Steering aids. Fins (especially if spiked) may also be used for protection. Some come in pairs, others are single.
- **Cold blood** Most fish stay the same temperature as the water surrounding them.
- **Internal skeleton** In sharks and rays, this is made of a tissue called cartilage. Other fish have skeletons of bone.

Do fish drink?

Sea fish drink a lot but excrete most of the salt. Freshwater fish absorb water through their skin, mouth, and gills

Flaps cover the gills

WHALE SHARK

Size surprise

As a group of animals, fish show an astonishing variation in size. The biggest is the 50 ft (15 m) whale shark. One of the tiniest is the stout infantfish, just ¼ in (7 mm) long.

STOUT INFANTFISH

Ripple effect

It's muscle power that enables a fish to swim. As a fish moves, a continuous ripple runs through muscles alongside its spine. This causes the fish's tail to waggle, which pushes the fish through the water as if it were driven by a paddle. The fins help with steering and braking. Some fish can do a reverse ripple and swim backward.

DOGFISH

Scales reduce friction in water

Dorsal fin prevents rolling

Tail, or caudal, fin

Paired pectoral fins aid stability

This is NOT a fish... it's a mammal

It's easy to forget that some of the animals that swim in the sea are mammals, more closely related to human beings than to the fish on which they often prey. Marine mammals include whales, seals, sea lions, dugongs, and manatees. All these animals give birth to live young and suckle their young on milk.

Take a close look. Whales don't even swim like fish.
A fish moves forward through the water by flexing its tail from side to side. Marine mammals (those with tails) use an up and down movement to propel themselves through the water.

Checklist for a mammal

- **Born live** Mammals give birth to live young.
- **Internal skeleton** A strong, bony skeleton provides a perfect framework for the body.
- **Suckling** The young are suckled on their mother's milk in the first months of life.
- **Lungs** Mammals breathe air, so marine mammals must come to the surface regularly.
- **Warm-blooded** Food is used to supply energy to keep a mammal's body warmer than the surrounding sea.
- **Parental care** Mammals care for their young for a long time after birth.

Manatees and dugongs
Also known as sea cows, these large marine mammals graze on seaweeds and seagrasses.

A whale can click and...

Whale song
Whales and dolphins are noisy creatures. Each animal may create a unique sound that it develops soon after birth. Whistles are used to "talk" to other whales and dolphins, and sometimes to locate a mate. The sound travels a long way in the ocean depths.

Dolphins find their way around, and locate prey, by using clicks and echoes. This is called echolocation, and it's incredibly effective. (It's similar to the way bats find their way around dark caves.) Using echolocation, a dolphin can tell not only the location of an object, but its size and shape as well.

I can see you!
As a dolphin swims, it sends out clicks that move through the water as vibrating waves. If something is swimming near a dolphin, it will block some of these waves and bounce them back. The dolphin hears these.

A ball of waxy tissue called the melon focuses clicks that are made in the nasal passages.

Blowhole

Nasal passage

Ear

Outgoing sounds

Returning waves travel through the dolphin's jaw to its ear.

Dolphins and porpoises
These are small, toothed whales. Most live in the ocean, but some live in freshwater.

Seals, sea lions, and walruses
These carnivores spend much of their lives in the water, but come on land to give birth.

Whales
The orca, or killer whale, is the largest member of the dolphin family.

13

SHARKS have all the *same* senses as human beings, and one that we *don't* have, giving them a distinct advantage in the water.

60

The fastest shark is a SHORTFIN MAKO, which can reach speeds of up to 60 mph (97 kph).

Sharks produce their own antibiotic, which protects them against bacterial and fungal infections.

6TH SENSE

A shark has a sixth sense that it uses to detect electrical fields. All living things give out weak electrical signals, and the shark has tiny jelly-filled canals on its snout that can detect them. Since boat engines and propellers emit these signals, too, sharks occasionally mistake these for prey—and attack! More usually though, hammerheads use their sixth sense to find fish hidden in the sand on the seafloor. Most sharks use it to home in on their prey when they're getting near enough to bite.

Sharks have powerful bites. In some species, each tooth can exert **132 lb** (60 kg) of pressure— enough to slice through the toughest flesh.

Many sharks lose between 8,000 and 20,000 teeth in a lifetime.

The whale shark is the biggest shark of all. A fully grown

SPINY DOGFISH,
a small species of shark, can live for up to **100 years.**

vISIOn

Most sharks have good eyesight and some can see in color. Many have large eyes that help collect light in the dim conditions under water. All sharks have eyelids, but they can't close them. Instead, certain sharks have membranes that slide over to protect their eyes from thrashing fish during feeding. The great white rolls its eyeballs around their sockets just before it bites prey, so at that moment it has to rely on other senses.

SMELL

The ability of sharks to detect a drop of blood from miles away is a bit of an exaggeration, but they can still detect fishy smells within several hundred yards. Sharks have a pair of nostrils under their snouts. As they move, water flows through the nostrils. When the shark picks up a scent it moves its head from side to side until it finds the direction the smell is coming from. Sharks also use this sense to find a mate, and may even use it to navigate.

Dogfish

Blacktip reef shark

Touch

Sharks feel through their skin and will often nose something or give it a test bite to make sure it is edible. A shark can also sense movement through a line of special cells along its sides called a lateral line. The cells pick up vibrations in the water, which the shark uses to pinpoint an object.

Lateral line

I hope you can't hear me.

HEARING

Even though they have no visible ears, sharks can hear under water. They are sensitive to low-frequency sounds and can tell which direction these come from over several miles.

The bull shark can live in **FRESH-** as well as **SEAWATER** and is sometimes found in rivers.

TASTE

Sharks have taste buds in their mouths but not on their tongues. Some sharks eat anything that comes along, others are more fussy and will reject things they don't like. Unfortunately for humans, they need to take a bite first.

specimen can reach **50 ft (15 m)**, which is longer than a bus.

Shark's skin
MAKES WAVES

A tight-fitting suit helps an *Olympic* swimmer such as Gary Hall Jr. to swim fast... but the tight fit is not the only secret.

Magnified shark's skin reveals its structure of tiny ridges called dermal denticles. They help the shark glide through the water with little resistance, because the water flows around each ridge without swirling, and so reduces drag.

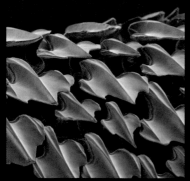

A close-up of the fastsuit fabric shows how it is woven in ridges similar to those of shark's skin. Manufacturers claim that these suits increase speed by three percent.

The fastest sharks can swim at speeds more than 10 times those of an Olympic athlete, and of course we will never be able to match them. In the quest for speedier swimming, however, a little help is available in the form of an amazing new swimsuit, called the "fastsuit."

Using new technology based on the study of shark skin, it's made from special material that helps swimmers to slip swiftly through the water. Wearing this suit may shave just a second or two off a swimmer's time, but that could be the tiny difference that wins a race.

Some yachts are now using paint on their hulls that is also based on shark-skin technology. It has the added advantage of making it more difficult for algae and barnacles to get a grip on the hull.

What do you do if you don't have teeth?

There are two types of whale:

Those with teeth

Those without teeth

TOOTHLESS

A massive blue whale needs lots to eat to stay healthy. It scoops up vast amounts of water, from which it filters out tiny fish and shrimplike creatures called krill. Inside its mouth are long fringes called baleen, which act as a strainer. A blue whale's baleen can filter out up to **8,000 lb** (**3,600 kg**) of krill a day.

WONDERS

GULP!

Feeding time

To feed, a whale opens its mouth and scoops up a mouthful of water. Then it closes its mouth almost completely and pushes out the water, through the baleen, with its tongue. Any krill and fish in the water are trapped by the baleen and swallowed.

Fish food

A blue whale eats **4 million krill** every day during the summer feeding season.

"Hi! I'm a krill."

0–1 trucks in 6 seconds!

No wonder krill is the most abundant animal on the planet. Twice a year, female krill lay around 2,500 eggs each. YUM!

The fin whale, like all rorquals, is a fast-feeder with a big appetite. It can take in enough water and krill to fill an average truck in barely 6 seconds. Imagine how big its mouth is, if it holds all of that.

Types of baleen feeders:

Northern right whale

Minke whale

Sei whale

Let's look at baleen

Baleen is made up of rows of bony plates, each with a hairy fringe to trap krill and other prey. These plates can be as long as 14 ft (4 m). Some whales have up to 700 hanging from each side of their upper jaws.

14 ft (4 m)

Bowhead and right whales—slow-movers with huge heads. They spend most of their time drifting around with their mouths open, ready to scoop up prey.

Rorquals—fast-movers that zoom in on their prey. Their throats can expand to take up great gulps of water. They include humpback and minke whales.

Gray whales—unlike the others, these feed mainly on the seabed, taking in mouthfuls of mud from which they filter out shrimp, starfish, and worms.

Heart of Darkness

You're a daredevil diver, plunging from the surface of the ocean to the deepest, most dangerous depths. As you descend through the ocean's five layers, or zones, it gets darker and darker, and colder and colder. You'll see all kinds of sea creatures on the way down (if you have a very powerful flashlight). But make sure to take the right diving gear, or you'll be crushed like a squeezed ping-pong ball by the huge pressure of water all around you.

In the extreme (and very dangerous) sport of freediving, divers descend as deep as 525 ft (160 m) with no breathing equipment. They have to hold their breath. At these depths, the pressure makes your lungs shrink to smaller than your fists.

Herring

Green turtle

660 ft (200 m)

Below the sunlit zone, you'll definitely need protection from the pressure. In 1934, William Beebe and Otis Barton dived to 3,028 ft (923 m) in a spherical diving vessel, the bathyscaphe. Today, you could dive to 2,000 ft (600 m) in a diving hard suit, a kind of pressure-resistant suit.

Sunlit zone

The sunlit zone is the top 660 ft (200 m) of the ocean, where it's sunny enough for water plants such as phytoplankton to grow. It's the busiest part of the ocean, since it's warm and there's plenty of food. You'll find hundreds of species of shark and other fish, as well as air-breathing animals like dolphins and turtles.

Silky shark

Wolf-fish

Pelagic sea cucumber

Giant octopus

3,300 ft (1,000 m)

For diving in the dark zone, you'll need a real submersible—a kind of mini-submarine that can cope with massive pressure. For the last 40 years, you could have taken *Alvin*, one of the world's best-known and busiest submersibles. It can carry three people and dive to a maximum depth of 15,000 ft (4,500 m).

Atolla jellyfish

Twilight zone

In the twilight zone, a little light from the sun filters through—but not enough to keep plants alive. You'll plunge past creatures such as squid and octopuses, jellyfish, and wolf-fish, and the mysterious swimming sea cucumber (a type of animal).

Gulper eel

13,000 ft (4,000 m)

20,000 ft (6,000 m)

35,795 ft (10,910 m)

If Mount Everest were turned upside down and put in the sea, it would reach this point.

← 29,000 ft (8,850 m)

Only one diving machine has been to the very bottom of the ocean—the *Trieste*, a bathyscaphe (meaning "deep boat"). It carried a two-man crew 35,795 ft (10,910 m) down to the deepest point in all the oceans, Challenger Deep, in 1960. Sadly, it's no longer in use.

It's time to abandon all-purpose *Alvin* and step inside a submersible specially designed for adventures in the abyss. The French-built *Nautile* or the Japanese *Shinkai 6500* are perfect for the job. The *Shinkai* is so tough it can survive the incredible pressure at 21,500 ft (6,500 m) below sea level.

Sperm whale

Dark zone

Once you're in the dark zone, there's no light except what comes from bioluminescent (glowing) deep-sea animals. You might bump into a giant squid as you descend, or a sperm whale on a trip from the surface to hunt for the squid. Some of the seabed lies at this depth, and deep-sea starfish and tube worms live there.

Deep-sea crab

Isopod

Abyssal zone

In most places, the abyssal zone is the deepest part of the ocean, so you'll hit the seabed. The ocean floor is covered with sticky, slimy ooze. You might see tiny f: like copepods, isopods, which look like giant woodlice, and glowing deep-sea fish. Animals here feed mainly on dead sea creatures that sink down from the zones above.

Anglerfish

Cusk eels

Hadal zone

Keep exploring, and you might find an undersea trench, where the ocean floor drops away into a huge crevasse. This extra-deep layer of water is called the hadal zone—from the Greek word for "hell." Even at these huge pressures, some sea creatures can survive. There are deep-sea jellyfish, clams, flatfish, and the strange-looking anglerfish.

NOW YOU *see* me...

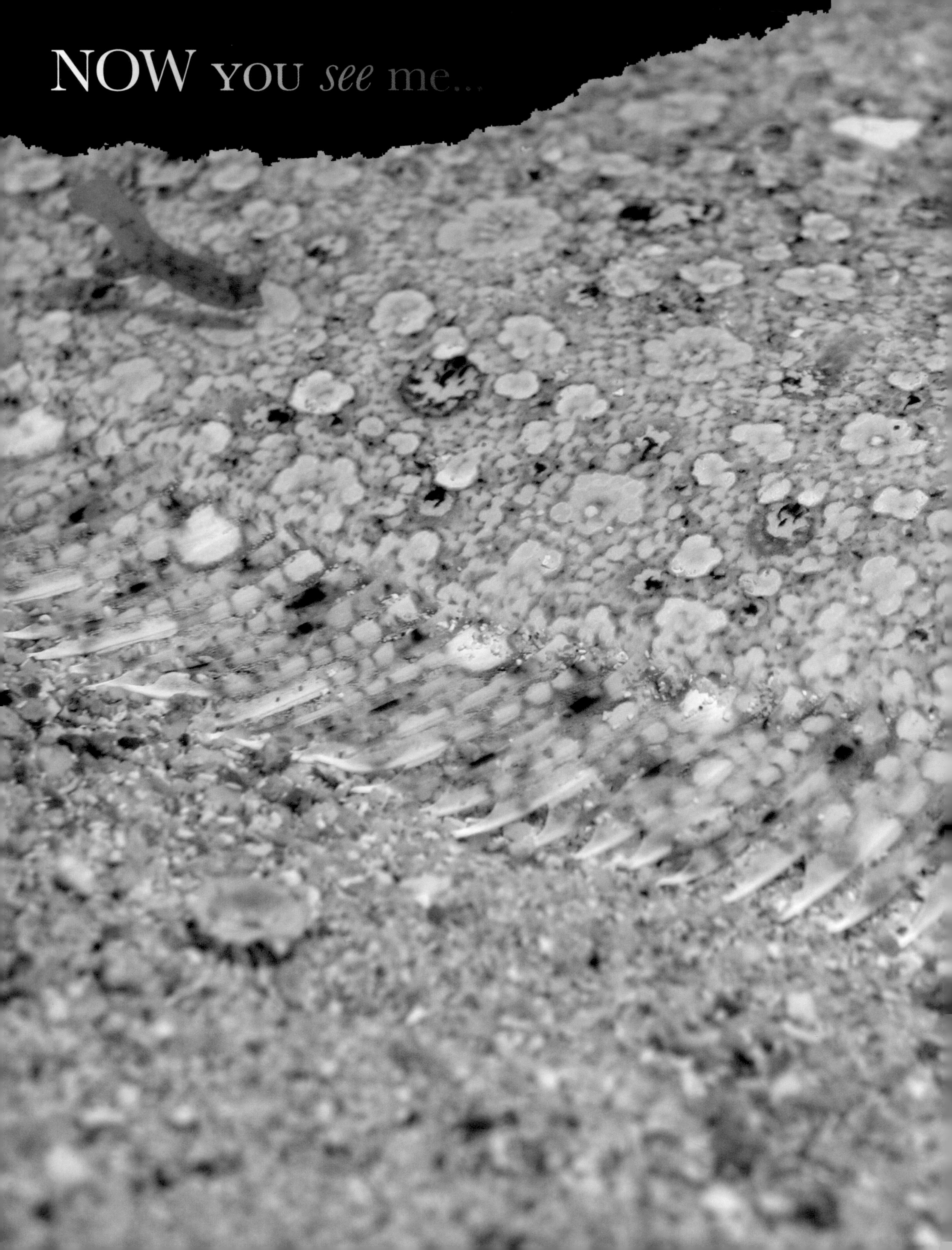

I AM A PEACOCK FLOUNDER HIDING IN SAND
OFF THE COAST OF TOBAGO IN THE CARIBBEAN.

Who's not the fairest of them all?

Deep down in the dark ocean, there's no need to be beautiful, which is a good thing if nature short-changed you in the looks department. We've made our top three choices in this underwater ugly pageant—now it's your turn to judge.

Scorpionfish

This contestant is not only ugly, but it's nasty, too—it has poisonous spines along its back.

Viperfish

No dentist could help this toothy creature—its fangs are so huge, they can't fit inside its gaping, glowing mouth.

Ribbon eel

A gruesome mouth, with nostril flaps above, give the ribbon eel a scary mug.

Rosy-lipped batfish

I'm much uglier than they are—just look at my nose!

All the makeup in the world wouldn't enhance this hopeful's charm, even on the dark ocean floor where it lives.

Gulper eel

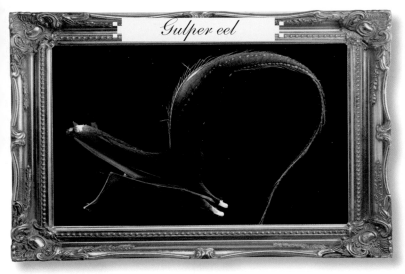

With a huge mouth at the end of a long, tapering body, this eel lacks pleasing proportions.

Blobfish

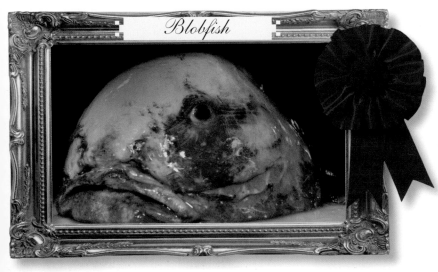

There's no point in this challenger toning up his muscles— most are like jelly. His body is like a squishy soccer ball.

Frogfish

This lumpy, spotted, wart-covered creature lives in the shallow water above coral reefs.

Hagfish

The ability to produce goo all over its body gives this entry its other alluring name: slime eel.

Ocean creatures live in many unusual places.

Salmon's skin
Hangers-on cause infections and even the death of the salmon.

Coral reef
Teeming with life, the reef provides food and shelter.

HERMIT CRAB
I move to a new home every time I grow.

Whale's skin
Hitchhikers hold on tight, gathering food from the water.

BARNACLE
My home is huge and always on the move.

Can you match these creatures to their homes?

Empty shell
This hard casing protects its occupant's soft abdomen.

SEA DRAGON
My home is a great hiding place.

LUGWORM
I dig to make my home.

Sandy burrow
Burrowers leave behind piles of sand on the surface as they make deep holes.

FISH LOUSE
I travel upriver, feeding on my home.

Sea grass
Creatures are hard to find among these long, wavy plants.

EMPEROR ANGEL FISH
My home is in warm waters.

FUELING *the* NATION

People have been killing and eating whales since prehistoric times. But between the 17th and 19th centuries whaling was a huge, multinational industry, and thousands of whales were killed each year. The reason? Oil from whales was a vital fuel, used in industry and to light people's homes. As a result, by the beginning of the 20th century some whale species had been hunted to the brink of extinction.

How to catch a whale

By the 19th century, hundreds of whaling ships were sailing the oceans for months on end in pursuit of sperm and right whales. When they spotted a whale, a team of men would set off from the main ship in a rowboat. They chased the whale and killed it with a harpoon attached to a rope, then towed its body back to their ship. A grisly process, called "cutting in," would then begin. The whale was cut up, and the blubber was peeled off in long strips and boiled in cauldrons, called try pots, to make whale oil.

The man who saved whales

In 1846, Abraham Gesner developed a process for refining a new liquid fuel, called kerosene, from coal. Kerosene became cheaper than whale oil and burned cleaner in lamps. Within 30 years it had largely replaced whale oil as a fuel. Whaling fleets became reduced in size, and thousands of whales were saved.

SAVE THE WHALES

Umbrella frames

Hairbrushes and combs

28

Oil, anyone?

John R. Jewitt was an Englishman who was held captive by the Nootka people on the northwest coast of North America from 1802 to 1805. In his memoir, he described how the Nootka would use "train oil" (whale oil) as a seasoning on their food—even on strawberries.

USES OF WHALE OIL

It was used in soap.

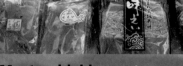

Train oil
Confusingly, whale oil was known as "train oil," but it had nothing to do with trains. The name came from an old Dutch word, meaning "tear."

Whale oil The most important whale oil in the 19th century was taken from the head of sperm whales. It was widely used.

Meat or blubber was eaten by Inuit and other northern peoples. It is still a popular food in Japan today.

USES OF BLUBBER

It was made into candles.

It was burned in lamps.

USES OF BALEEN

Corsets

USES OF AMBERGRIS

Baleen whales, such as the bowhead and right whale, were hunted for the baleen plates in their mouths.

Stiff brushes

Ambergris is a dark waxy substance produced in the intestine of the sperm whale. In the 19th century it was used to make expensive perfumes.

29

What's inside a shell?

Creatures with soft bodies need protection to prevent them from being injured by other animals. Some have developed stings or poisonous skin to keep from being eaten. Others have grown hard, impenetrable shells. When danger threatens, they pull all their soft parts back inside the shell and slam the door shut.

☀ Scallop

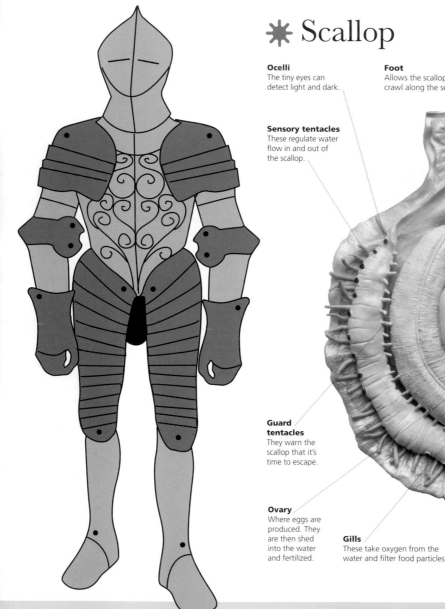

Ocelli
The tiny eyes can detect light and dark.

Foot
Allows the scallop to crawl along the seabed.

Hinge ligament
This holds the two shell-parts apart.

Palps
These sort out food particles and pass them to the mouth.

Sensory tentacles
These regulate water flow in and out of the scallop.

Digestive gland
Digests food taken in by the palps.

Heart
The heart pumps blood to the scallop's tissues and gills.

Guard tentacles
They warn the scallop that it's time to escape.

Muscle
One muscle closes the shell quickly and another holds it shut for long periods of time.

Ovary
Where eggs are produced. They are then shed into the water and fertilized.

Gills
These take oxygen from the water and filter food particles.

Kidneys
These extract waste products from the blood.

Mantle fold
A fold of skin that surrounds the soft body.

Intestines
Waste food passes along this tube before it is expelled.

Humans have internal skeletons, which leave the skin and muscles at risk of damage. During battles over the centuries, people have tried to protect themselves. Medieval knights wore heavy metal suits of armor, which made them look like huge metal lobsters.

Scallop at the gallop
Scallops, mussels, and clams are bivalve mollusks. They have two shell-parts that are hinged together, but scallops can never completely close their shells. Although they prefer to stay on the seabed, scallops can swim by vigorously squirting water out through their shell-parts and clapping the parts together.

✳ Sea urchin

Radial nerve
This nerve passes instructions to the feet and spines.

Urchin shell
The shell is made up of hard interlocking plates.

Tube feet
Each foot ends in a sucker to help grip on to surfaces.

Muscle
The muscles operate the movement of the teeth while grazing.

Mouth
This is under the shell.

Sieve plate
Seawater is drawn in here to maintain internal pressure.

Rectum
Waste material passes along here and leaves through the anus.

Canal complex
This canal connects the circulatory system with the sieve plate.

Ring canal
This is filled with fluid and carries substances around the body.

Spines
These can move through a ball-and-socket joint.

Tooth
Urchins have five teeth that keep on growing.

Intestine
Food is digested here.

✳ Nautilus

Hood
This covers the entrance when the nautilus draws back into its shell.

Tentacles
There are up to 90 sticky tentacles arranged in rows.

Inner tentacles
These pass food to the mouth.

Funnel
Water is pushed out of the funnel and propels the nautilus backward.

Tongue
This is covered with a number of small teeth.

Gills
These take oxygen out of water drawn in by the funnel.

Digestive gland
Food is broken down here.

Empty chamber
As the nautilus grows, the old body chamber is sealed and filled with gas.

Siphuncle
This regulates the amount of gas in the chambers.

Gonads
These contain either male or female reproductive organs.

Crop
Food is stored here before it enters the stomach.

Heart
This pumps blood around the nautilus.

Kidney
Removes waste products from the blood.

Intestine
Food is digested here or passed on to be expelled.

Prickly customer
Spines are a good way to stop something from nibbling you, and sea urchins are well-equipped. Between the spines, sea urchins have rows of tube feet, which they use to move along the seabed. The mouth is on the underside of the shell. Urchins also have tiny poison pincers between their spines.

Rooms to rent
A nautilus lives in a spiral shell that is divided into many chambers. Its body occupies only the outer chamber. As it grows bigger, a new chamber is added on. The old chambers are filled with gas, which helps the nautilus to float. The nautilus swims by jet propulsion, but can only go backward.

What's inside a fish?

All fish have an internal skeleton, similar to ours. Most fish, including cod and goldfish, have a bone skeleton. In sharks and rays the skeleton is made of cartilage, which is lighter and more flexible.

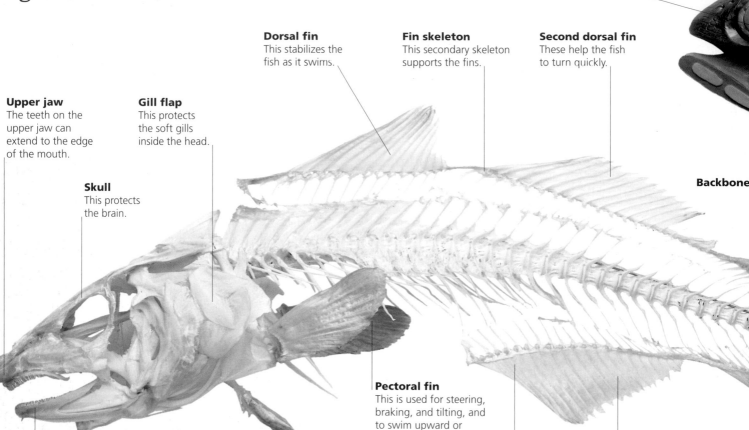

Eye
Most fish have good eyesight and many can see colors.

Dorsal fin
This stabilizes the fish as it swims.

Fin skeleton
This secondary skeleton supports the fins.

Second dorsal fin
These help the fish to turn quickly.

Upper jaw
The teeth on the upper jaw can extend to the edge of the mouth.

Gill flap
This protects the soft gills inside the head.

Skull
This protects the brain.

Backbone

Lower jaw
This acts as a chin and supports the lower teeth.

Pectoral fin
This is used for steering, braking, and tilting, and to swim upward or backward.

Lower fin skeleton
This supports the fins underneath the fish.

Front anal fin
This is used to stabilize the fish while swimming.

The art of swimming

To move in the water, all fish need a mechanism to help them sink or float. Bony fish have a swim bladder, which allows them to remain in the same position in the water without moving forward. They use their tail fins for propulsion and their other fins for maneuvering. Cartilaginous fish do not have a swim bladder. They have to keep moving to stay at the same level in the water. These fish have wide pectoral fins that help them raise their heads as they swim.

Most fish swim in a series of S-shaped waves, as if they are wriggling through the water.

First, the fish pushes its head to one side. The rest of the body begins to move in the same direction.

As the wave of movement passes along the fish, the tail swings out, pushing the fish forward at the same time.

Brain
This coordinates signals from the sense organs and tells the body how to react.

Gills
The gills are thin membranes that have a rich blood supply. They absorb oxygen from the water.

Spinal cord
This runs through the backbone and sends messages from the brain to the muscles and organs.

Kidney
Removes unwanted substances from the blood.

Muscle
Solid and powerful muscles help the fish swim against strong currents.

Lateral line
This line of fluid-filled cells helps the fish detect movements in the water.

Heart
The heart pumps blood to the gills, from where it is circulated around the rest of the body.

Soft-rayed dorsal fin
Not all fish have a second or third dorsal fin.

Swim bladder
Bony fish can adjust the amount of gas this contains, allowing them to float without using their fins.

Intestines
Food passes into the stomach and then into the intestines, which is where nutrients are absorbed into the blood.

Ovary
Female fish produce their eggs here, ready for shedding into the water to be fertilized by a male fish.

Rear anal fin
Some fish have only one anal fin.

Tail vertebrae

Caudal fin
The tail fin acts as a rudder.

Fish inside out

Most of a fish's internal organs are in the lower half of its body. The rest is dense muscle, which powers the fish through the water. Its body and fins are covered in a tough but flexible skin. The skin is then covered in a protective layer of scales.

Breathing under water

Fish get the oxygen they need by gulping in water and pushing it over their gills. The gills take oxygen out of the water and release carbon dioxide back into it. The water then flows out through flaps on the fish's head.

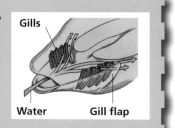

Gills

Water

Gill flap

The fish then begins to move its head the other way, starting a new wave along its body.

The fish flicks its tail to follow the direction of the head, pushing the fish forward, ready for the next change of direction.

A LONG WAY HOME

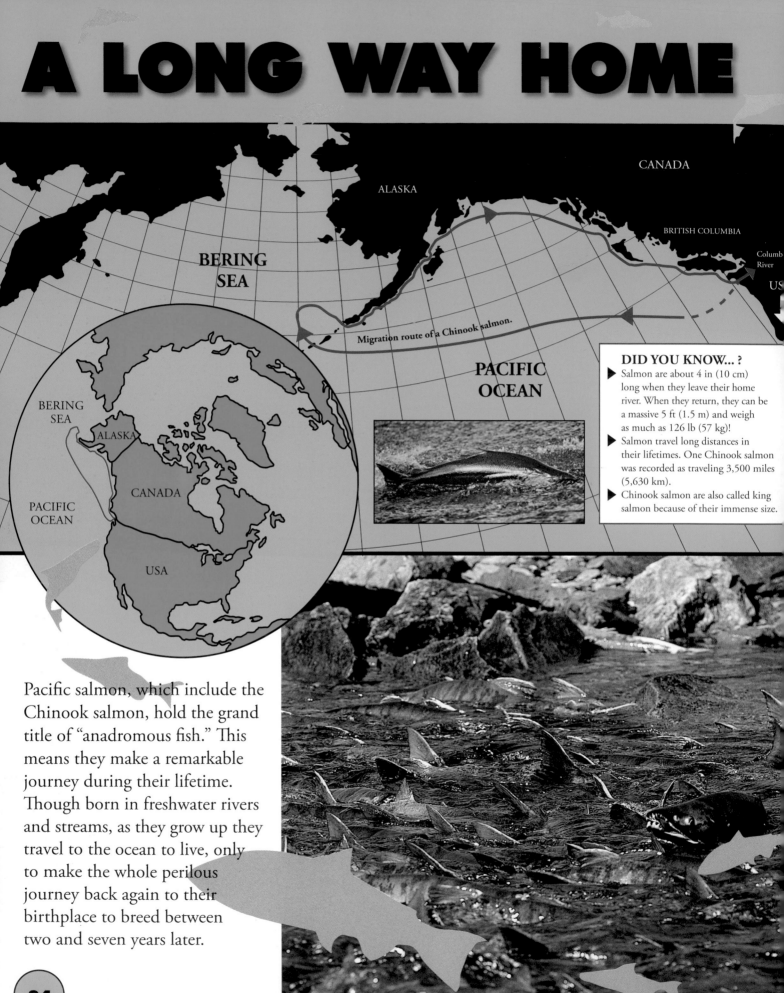

CANADA

ALASKA

BRITISH COLUMBIA

BERING
SEA

Columb
River

US

Migration route of a Chinook salmon.

PACIFIC
OCEAN

BERING
SEA

ALASKA

CANADA

PACIFIC
OCEAN

USA

DID YOU KNOW...?

▶ Salmon are about 4 in (10 cm) long when they leave their home river. When they return, they can be a massive 5 ft (1.5 m) and weigh as much as 126 lb (57 kg)!

▶ Salmon travel long distances in their lifetimes. One Chinook salmon was recorded as traveling 3,500 miles (5,630 km).

▶ Chinook salmon are also called king salmon because of their immense size.

Pacific salmon, which include the Chinook salmon, hold the grand title of "anadromous fish." This means they make a remarkable journey during their lifetime. Though born in freshwater rivers and streams, as they grow up they travel to the ocean to live, only to make the whole perilous journey back again to their birthplace to breed between two and seven years later.

1 I'm a female Chinook salmon. Now that I am mature, I am ready to travel the long distance home with the rest of the salmon to spawn (lay eggs and have them fertilized). No one knows how we find our way back—the ocean currents, the stars, the Sun, the Earth's magnetic field, our keen sense of smell? We just know we must return.

2 Orcas (killer whales) chase us, but many manage to escape. If we sense sea lions nearby, we swim away—fast! I am scarred and scratched where I have narrowly missed being caught and eaten!

3 We spend two months traveling, following the ocean currents and covering up to 35 miles (56 km) a day. On the way we eat small fish, shrimp, and squid to gain weight and become stronger.

LET ME GO!

4 Once I reach the mouth of the river, I use my stored-up energy to swim against the current—no time to stop and eat any more. My scales darken now that I'm in freshwater, although male scales brighten. Fishermen gather here waiting to pounce. A hook gets me, but I twist and leap until I'm free. Some are not so lucky...

5 I use my keen sense of smell to find my way upriver. At the hydroelectric dam, humans have built a special fish ladder for all kinds of salmon to leap up. Those that miss the ladder die from exhaustion as they try to find another way over the dam.

Fish use the ladder to scale the dam rung by rung.

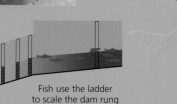

6 Amazingly, I still have enough energy to leap up rapids with a flick of my powerful tail. At the top, bears lie in wait for us. They may only take one bite out of a fish before discarding it for another. Danger comes from eagles, too—they swoop down as we leap and carry us off.

7 I make it through some cloudy water, churned up by logging and dredging. If the silt particles clog my gills, I won't be able to take in oxygen and will die. I narrowly avoid being poisoned by agricultural and industrial waste and crushed by fallen logs and rocks.

8 I'm exhausted when I arrive home. I pick the place for my nest (redd) carefully. I need a pool where there are rocks to hide behind, rippling water to provide oxygen for my brood, and a gravel bed to protect my eggs from predators.

9 I make hollows for my eggs—all 8,000 of them—by turning on my side and swishing my tail back and forth. I lay my eggs, then my male partner fertilizes them with milt (sperm). I sweep gravel over them for protection.

10 My one chance to reproduce is now over and I die a few weeks after spawning.

11 My babies hatch under the gravel and feed from their yolk sac before swimming away a few months later.

WHAT AM

IS
THIS WHAT
THE UNDERWATER
WORLD WOULD LOOK
LIKE IF YOU WERE AS
SMALL AS A SHRIMP?
CAN YOU GUESS
WHAT EACH
PICTURE SHOWS?

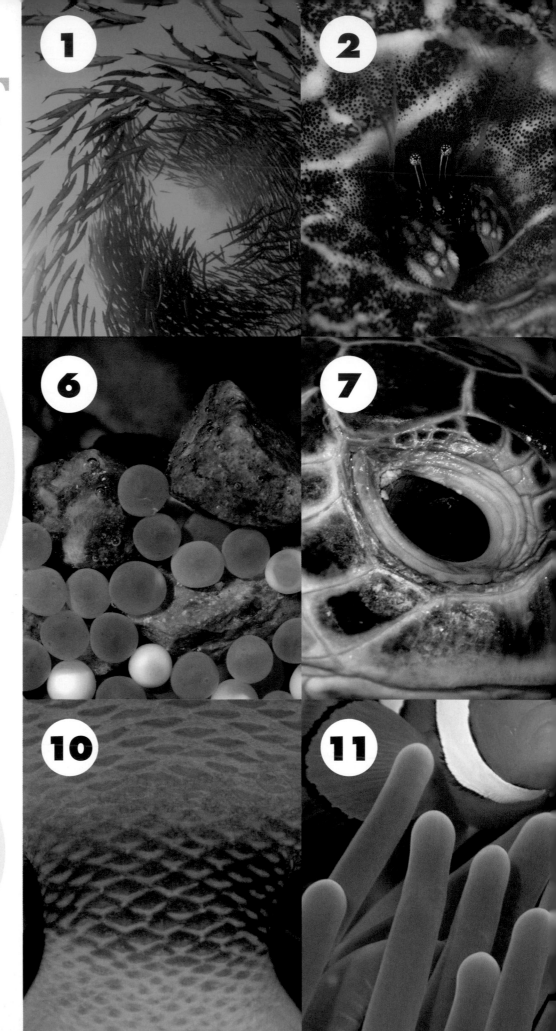

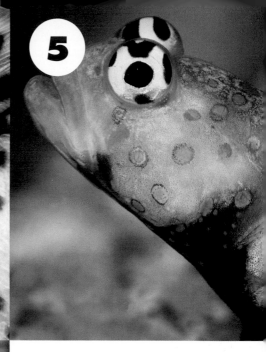

1. SCHOOL OF BARRACUDA
2. HERMIT CRAB IN WORM BURROW
3. GREAT WHITE SHARK
4. FIN OF BLACK-SPOTTED SWEETLIP FISH
5. ORANGE-SPOTTED SHRIMP GOBY
6. SEA TROUT EGGS
7. A TURTLE'S EYE
8. GIANT CLAM'S SIPHON
9. GILDED PIPEFISH
10. TAIL OF AN ANGEL FISH
11. CLOWNFISH IN ANEMONE
12. SEA LILIES (CRINOIDS)
13. MOON JELLYFISH
14. SPINES OF A LIONFISH

50 VOLTS

ELECTRIC CATFISH
This fish just crackles with energy all over—almost its entire body is wired up to discharge electricity. The catfish adjusts both the length and the strength of its discharges according to whether it's navigating in the dark, searching for prey, or firing off a stunning blast at an enemy.

200 VOLTS

TORPEDO RAY
When ancient Greeks and Romans had a migraine, the doctor prescribed… a torpedo ray. This fish has glands near its head that produce electrical currents, so a live ray was held to the patient's forehead in the belief that its electricity bolt would cure the headache. In fact, a torpedo ray's charge causes numbness, so maybe the remedy really worked.

50 VOLTS

STARGAZER
Low-voltage but still with a lot of spark, this little fish spends most of its life buried in the seafloor. Try not to step on it—its electrical charge (fired from behind its eyes) will really make you jump.

argghh…

THE SHOCKING

Some fish have special cells in their bodies that produce strong *electric discharges.* They can use these to electrocute other fish and to give humans a nasty jolt.

Discover *ELECTRIFYING* facts to STUN your imagination!

TRUTH

ELECTRIC EEL

The most powerful shock comes from the electric eel, which isn't an eel at all. In fact, it's an 8-ft- (2.5-m-) long fish belonging to the group known as knifefish. In its snakelike body, which is more tail than head, the electric eel has three pairs of electrical organs, like sets of batteries. To locate prey, it sends out weak electrical signals that help it to sense its environment, a bit like radar. This is a great help when you live, like this fish does, in dark, muddy rivers where visibility is poor. To make life even dimmer, the electric eel also has really bad eyesight that gets worse as it ages. Electricity doesn't light up this creature's surroundings, but it does keep it in touch with its world.

High voltage
650 VOLTS

... a whopping discharge hits victims with about 3–5 times the voltage they'd get from a standard electrical outlet.

It's a fish-eat-fish world

in the ocean. Look at these fishy pairs and choose which ones are friends and which ones are foes. Do these unlikely pairings help each other out or does one of them get eaten by the other for dinner?

Leatherback turtle and jellyfish

TAKE A BITE
Instead of teeth, the leatherback turtle has backward-pointing spines in its throat, which are used to puncture a passing jellyfish before swallowing it.

Food

Man-o-war fish and Portuguese man-o-war

Friends

DEADLY TENTACLES
The man-o-war fish can happily swim among the stinging tentacles of the Portuguese man-o-war. In doing so, the fish encourages other fish to swim near, providing food for its protector.

Friend or food?

Remoras and shark

FRIENDS that feed...
Remoras bravely attach themselves with suckers to the sides of a shark to hitch a ride. They feed on the shark's skin parasites and scraps of food left over from the shark's meals. Scientists have yet to find a shark eating a remora.

What's for dinner?

How about takeout tonight?

Leave some for me, boys!

Hermit crab and sea anemone

Friends

MOVEABLE SHELL
A hermit crab is protected by the sea anemone hitching a ride on its shell. In return, the anemone gets scraps of food from the crab and is able to move around.

Imperial shrimp and sea cucumber

Friends

ALONG FOR THE RIDE
An imperial shrimp hitches a ride on the back of a sea cucumber moving from one feeding ground to another. The sea cucumber is unharmed but gets no benefit from its hitchhiker.

MMMMM!
You look tasty.

Shark and octopus

Food

SIZE MATTERS
Octopuses often fall prey to a hungry shark. However, sharks need to be wary of a lurking large octopus, which could ensnare a shark with its long tentacles and then devour it.

Orca whale and blue whale

Food

PACK HUNTERS
Undeterred by the vast size of a blue whale, orca whales will sometimes work together to separate a mother from its calf. Once successful, the orcas attack the helpless calf with great ferocity.

Pacific cleaner shrimp and grouper

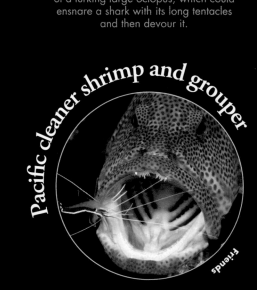

Friends

JAWS OF DEATH
A Pacific cleaner shrimp swims unharmed into the open mouth of a grouper. Why? The shrimp eats the parasites, cleaning out the grateful grouper's mouth.

Cleaning stations

ON A CORAL REEF THERE are particular spots where fish line up to be cleaned by other fish. The "cleaner" fish eat skin parasites and diseased and dead skin and remove mucus from the client fish. Both fish benefit: one gets a good meal; the other gets a free grooming session!

Blue-striped grunt fish

Ready for a cleaning, Madam?

Yes please, these parasites are a pain!

The **client** asks for attention by opening its mouth and flapping its fins.

Four-eyed butterfly fish

The **cleaner** signals it is ready to do its job.

Personal cleaner

This shrimp might be a tasty appetizer for the moray eel, but it is actually quite safe as it services its fierce client. It gives the eel's skin a good going over, cleaning off any parasites.

No, those jaws are not about to shut; instead this huge grouper allows the wrasse to pick bits of stale food out of its mouth. Cleaner wrasses have a bright "uniform" of black-and-white stripes.

GLOW-IN-THE-DARK

70%

of free-swimming, dark-zone animals produce their own light.

Now you see me, now you don't

Some animals, such as squid, have photophores—light-producing organs—on the undersides of their bodies. Squid use these to hide from predators looking upward to spot silhouettes of fish for dinner. By turning on their photophores, they illuminate their bodies so the predator thinks it can see sunlight rather than a squid.

This flask is filled with tiny algae that use bioluminescence. Most marine organisms produce a blueish-green light because it travels farther through water than other colors.

IN THE GLOOMY DEPTHS of the ocean

it is easy to hide from your enemies, but it is just as easy to bump into one. Animals that live in these dark waters have their own special light sources that they can turn on and off. The way they make this light is called

BIOLUMINESCENCE.

Bioluminescence is a chemical reaction that uses a compound called luciferin. There are probably several reasons why these animals glow in the dark. In some species it may be used for communication, in others to attract a mate. Some squid and crustaceans expel a cloud of bioluminescent material to repel predators. Light can also be used to lure prey.

Go away!

Other animals use bioluminescence to confuse predators. Most comb jellies can eject a cloud of bioluminescent particles to distract anything trying to eat them. Other jellyfish have a row of photophores along the edge of their bell that they flash to startle predators, or they detach glowing tentacles as decoys.

Sparkling seas

Sailors have often reported the waves around their boat sparkling as they go through the water at night. This is caused by millions of tiny algae called dinoflagellates that make the water look red in the daytime, but flash if disturbed. They also light up if they sense a predator—the flashing alerts a bigger predator who, hopefully, will gobble up the one eating the algae.

Over here!

Instead of roaming around looking for your prey, another solution is to get your prey to come to you. Many predatory species, such as anglerfish, use a dangling light or a glowing spot inside their mouths to attract unsuspecting fish. Glowing lights are also used to find a mate. The flashes indicate whether the fish is male or female and whether it is ready for mating.

SURVIVING

1,650 ft
500 m

Down, down, down in the depths of the ocean it is very dark and cold. The immense pressure would kill a human being. Food is scarce. Tasty morsels are few and far between. Aside from that, it's lovely, and a surprisingly wide range of creatures survive there.

3,300 ft
1,000 m

Light

Rod

Daggerlike teeth

5,000 ft
1,500 m

6,500 ft
2,000 m

The fisherman
This strange-looking creature is an anglerfish—it catches its prey with a rod and bait, like a human angler. The rod is a long spine that projects from the fish's head. On the end is a lump that produces a blue-green light that acts as the bait. The anglerfish wiggles the light about to lure other fish to come close, then snaps them up in its powerful jaws and swallows them whole.

8,000 ft
2,500 m

The **Empire State Building** in New York City is 1,472 ft (449 m) tall.

GONE FISHING

THE DEEP

Invisibility cloak
This hatchet fish has a row of light-producing organs along each side of its body that point downward. The lights camouflage the fish because, from below, they make it invisible against the faint light coming from the surface above.

Toothy!
Big teeth are an advantage in the deep, but the ferocious-looking fangtooth has taken this to the extreme. In relation to its body size, it has the longest teeth of any fish. Its bottom fangs are so long that they slip into special sockets in the roof of the fish's mouth when the jaw closes.

SURVIVAL CHECK LIST
- Lightweight skeleton, jellylike tissues, and reduced muscle
- Slow lifestyle
- Large mouth
- Expandable stomach for big prey
- Long, sharp teeth for eating almost anything
- Dull colors for camouflage
- Light for attracting prey

Seabed vacuum
Deep-sea cucumbers are scavengers that spend their time vacuuming up plankton and decaying organic matter from the water. They also scoop up seabed sediment into their mouths with their tube feet. They are almost colorless but glow with bioluminescent light.

Fearsome hunter
The bizarre and hideous viperfish is mostly head and teeth, with rows of light-producing organs along its sides and belly. It is one of the fiercest predators of the deep, swimming toward its victims at high speed and impaling them on its sharp, fanglike teeth.

Who's the DADDY?

Some fish may produce more than two million eggs each year. Many are left to float around in the ocean, and it is pure luck whether they survive and hatch or become a meal for another sea creature. In some cases, the parents have fewer eggs but take better care of them. Perhaps surprisingly, it is sometimes the males who take on most of this egg-minding responsibility.

Dad's pregnant!
This pregnant seahorse isn't female but male. Roles are reversed in the seahorse world, since it's the males that have pouches. The female lays eggs into the pouch, where the male keeps them safe. After 8 to 10 days, the male gives birth by squeezing the babies out of a small opening.

Home guard

This stickleback is very committed to protecting his eggs. Not only does he build a cozy nest in which one or more females lay the eggs, but for two weeks he doesn't eat as he stays nearby chasing away any intruders until the eggs hatch.

A mouthful

This jawfish appears to be devouring his offspring, but he's no cannibal. He's what is called a mouthbrooder. For safekeeping, a male jawfish collects all the eggs laid by the female and holds them in his mouth. There's no dinner for him until the fish hatch and swim away.

Wrapped up

Look closely and you'll see this cryptic anglerfish has its eggs wrapped up in his tail. The female lays eggs onto the male's tail and then he folds over his tail and carries them around until they hatch.

head

tail

ONE OF THE MOST COMMON injuries caused by a sea creature happens when someone steps on a sea urchin. Most incidents result in mild to severe pain or infection, but symptoms are much more serious if a bit of the spine gets left in the wound.

The sea wasp, also known as the box jellyfish, is arguably the most deadly of all marine creatures. Found in Australian estuaries and coastal waters, it can be as large as a bucket, with tentacles 10 ft (3 m) long. Each one of these shoots a lethal poison into the skin of any creature that touches it. This poison can cause excruciating pain, breathing problems, cardiac arrest, and even death in human beings.

Fire coral isn't coral at all—it looks like coral, and it's found on coral reefs, but it's actually an animal related to the jellyfish. This creature has small, almost-invisible tentacles, which divers can brush accidentally. Within five or 10 minutes, their skin will sting and burn, and an itchy rash appears. Sometimes, they feel sick, and notice swelling in their lymph glands. Once in a while, contact can cause a severe allergic reaction.

Banded sea snakes produce a poison several times more powerful than cobra venom. Active at night, they swim close to shore. Most of their victims are fishermen, who get bitten when they try to untangle the snakes from large fishing nets. The bite is small and relatively painless, so it sometimes goes unnoticed until it's too late.

danger

Some marine creatures **defend** themselves in ways that are either

There are more than 250 species of ray in our seas, and among these are 10 families of stingray. These all have a spine or barb at the base of their tails that contains highly toxic venom. In 2006, Australian naturalist Steve Irwin was killed by a stingray barb that pierced his heart.

The blue-ringed octopus kills by injecting a powerful poison into its victim—this poison can kill a human being within 15 minutes. Luckily, this creature is not particularly aggressive, and it will attack only if it's provoked or stepped on. The blue rings that give this octopus its name do not usually stand out, but when it gets alarmed, they suddenly become bright and iridescent to warn off enemies.

People do far more harm to sharks than sharks do to people. A few species of shark have been known to attack swimmers and divers. Probably the most famous of these is the great white shark, with its terrifying row of huge teeth. It usually preys on large marine animals, but it can occasionally mistake a person for one of these.

Second biggest of all starfish, the crown of thorns grows up to 25 in (60 cm) in diameter. It has 13–16 arms, each one covered in sharp, poisonous spines. If you step on one, your foot will sting and swell, staying swollen for days or even weeks—your lymph glands might swell, too, and you could experience nausea and vomiting.

Well camouflaged against the underwater stone that inspired its name, the stone fish is highly venomous, with sharp spines that can pierce a leather shoe. Untreated, its poison not only causes excruciating pain that can last for months, but it can also kill living tissue, resulting in amputation, and even death.

in the water!

 DEADLY or ! PAINFUL and IR ITATING.

Things
that sting

These jellyfish (and their wobbly look-alike, the Portuguese man-o-war) seem too fragile to be scary. But their long tentacles can pack a poisonous sting. Death by jellyfish is not unheard of, although not all jellyfish are dangerous. Found in seas around the world, they sometimes gather in vast numbers, called "blooms."

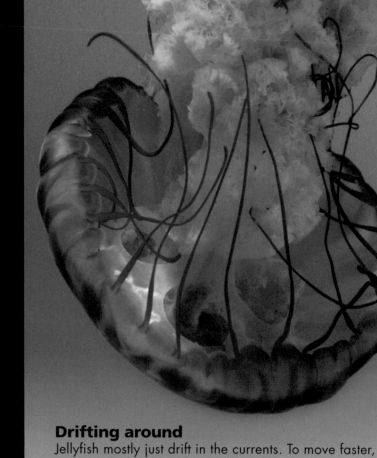

JUST FRIENDS

Supersafe
Not victims, but friends—these small fish have not been killed by a deadly jellyfish. Because of a protective mucus on their bodies, they can touch the tentacles and remain unharmed. A jellyfish provides a good refuge from enemies. Who would dare to fish them out from there?

Drifting around
Jellyfish mostly just drift in the currents. To move faster, they swim by expanding and contracting their bodies, which forces water out and propels them along.

The venom of the box jellyfish can kill in minutes.

WARNING!
If you see a sign like this one on the beach, it means "Watch out, there are jellyfish around." Even dead jellyfish washed up on the sands can still sting.

 Ageless Jellyfish have been floating (and stinging) in the oceans for more than 500 million years. That means they first appeared on Earth long before the dinosaurs. And they're still here!

 Brainless When brains were handed out, jellyfish didn't get any. However, they do have a primitive nervous system that allows them to detect nearby prey and react to danger.

Lion's mane

With trails of stinging tentacles that can reach more than 100 ft (30 m) in length, the lion's mane jellyfish is not something to tangle with. If a fish collides with the jellyfish, the tentacles immediately release a paralzing poison. The jellyfish then eats its helpless prey.

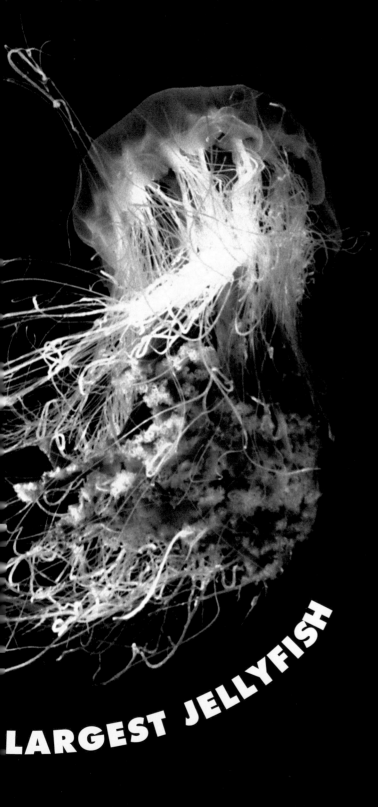

LARGEST JELLYFISH

Portuguese man-o-war

This poisonous stinger, closely related to the jellyfish, is a colony of small marine animals. They cluster together under a gas-filled bag that carries them over the oceans.

Before discharge
- surface cell
- coiled thread
- stinging cell

After discharge
- uncoiled thread
- barbs

Deadly darts

Jellyfish and man-o-war tentacles (see close-up photo) contain tiny stinging cells. When touched, each cell fires a poisoned, barbed thread, like a mini harpoon, that pierces the victim's skin.

Eyeless Jellyfish don't have an actual head or eyes, but they do have clusters of light-sensing cells scattered around the rim of the "bell." A jellyfish can tell light from dark and swim toward the light.

Gutless And heartless, boneless, and bloodless! A jellyfish has none of the usual body parts—it seems like little more than a bag of water. Yet these creatures can strike terror into swimmers and divers.

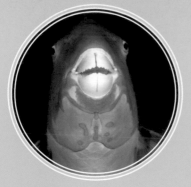

Who's a pretty boy?

Parrotfish are *tropical,* sand-building fish. They live in and around **coral reefs** in the *Red Sea,* the *Indian* and *Pacific oceans,* and in waters off the *Caribbean.* They get their name from the way their numerous TIGHTLY PACKED TEETH are fused together TO FORM A TYPE OF **"beak"** that is very similar TO THAT of a *parrot.* Some species are *huge.*

A parrotfish leads a busy life, although much of its day involves grazing on coral gardens. Let's take a look.

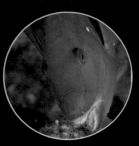

Coral The "beak" proves an effective tool to scrape algae, their main food, from coral. By doing this, they play an important role in **stopping coral reefs from becoming choked with greenery.**

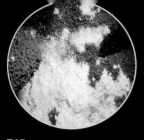

Waste Bumphead parrotfish swallow coral rock when they feed. This is ground up by special teeth and excreted, undigested, as sand. Such sand has **helped to create Caribbean beaches.**

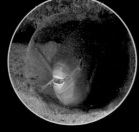

Night safety Some parrotfish species wrap themselves in special "pajamas" at night by secreting a transparent envelope of mucus around themselves. It's thought that this **helps to hide the fish.**

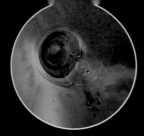

Clean up Like many other reef fish, parrotfish use the services of cleaner shrimp to remove parasites and dead bits of skin from their mouths and eyes. This **helps to prevent infection and disease.**

Boy or girl? As young parrotfish mature, they may change sex. If a group's male dies, one of the females is likely to change sex (and coloring) to become male. But it may **change back if needed.**

Yummy Cooked parrotfish is delicious to eat and also good for you. However, overfishing of parrotfish can widely **disrupt the delicate balance of species on the reef.**

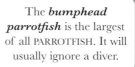

The *bumphead parrotfish* is the largest of all PARROTFISH. It will usually ignore a diver.

Prickly character

THE PORCUPINE FISH plays a sharp trick on predators. When in danger, it blows itself up into a spiked ball—enough to spoil anyone's appetite.

By filling my stomach with water, I swell up to two or three times my usual size. As my skin stretches, all my spines stand on end.

Deflated

At rest, the slow-moving porcupine fish keeps its spines flat against its body. Looks like an easy catch...

... but would-be predators need to be careful.

If it **DOES** get caught unawares, the porcupine fish will inflate itself in a predator's mouth. Ouch!

I may look sw et and innoc nt

Getting blown up

To blow itself up, the porcupine fish doesn't puff, it pumps. This draws water into its stretchy stomach, which expands like a balloon within a few seconds. As the tummy fills up, the backbone curves. When the danger has passed, the porcupine fish deflates.

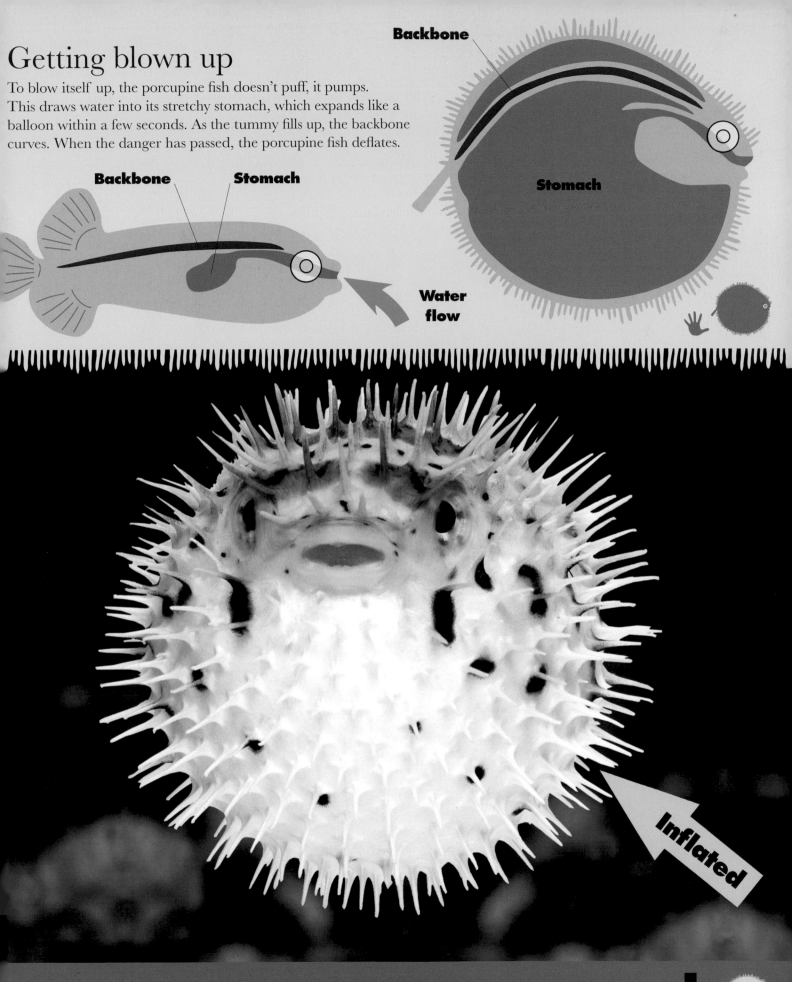

Backbone

Backbone

Stomach

Stomach

Water flow

Inflated

... but on't make me ungry!

Coming up for AIR

A whale's "nostrils," or blowholes, are on top of its head. The whale sucks in or blows out air very quickly. The exhaled air blasts out at around **300 mph** (480 kph). Moisture in the breath turns to water droplets, which spray up to **30 ft** (9 m) into the air.

A whale couldn't drown, could it?

It sounds crazy, but it is possible. Although sea mammals such as whales and dolphins spend all their lives in water, they still need to breathe air to gain the oxygen they need. Unlike fish, which have gills to take in oxygen from the water, mammals have lungs like us. Whales and dolphins normally pop up to the surface every few minutes for good deep breaths. They can stay down longer during dives.

Just before a whale dives, flaps close tightly over its blowholes to keep out the water.

A whale's breath smells **PUNGENT** and *fishy*.

Brain control

Our brains automatically control our breathing, even when we are asleep. Whales and dolphins need to be more aware of controlling their breathing by their own efforts. They can't drop off into a deep sleep because their breathing would stop. Instead, they take short naps while they float, or swim slowly, just below the surface. As a whale or dolphin rests, half its brain stays awake, to remind it to breathe now and then. The other half enjoys a little snooze!

TAKE A BREATH

How long can you hold your breath? Perhaps **30 seconds?** A champion breath-holder among sea mammals is Cuvier's beaked whale. It can last without breathing for an astonishing **85 minutes**, as it dives down to depths of around **6,500 ft (2,000 m).**

Freediver Tanya Streeter can hold her breath for a record-breaking **six minutes!**

Air supply

Whales such as orcas (below), which live in polar regions, risk having their air supply cut off when the seas freeze over in winter. They have to find gaps in the ice where they can come up to breathe. The huge bowhead whale found in Arctic waters has fewer worries than most. With its massive skull, it can headbutt holes in ice more than 12 in (30 cm) thick.

Phew... back at the surface. I could use some air!

SAVED BY SLIME

Pale, eel-like, and almost blind, the HAGFISH has an unusual way of defending itself. When attacked, *it oozes slime,* which swells into a gel when mixed with seawater. This forms a cocoon around the fish.

Slime from hagfish

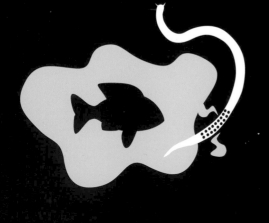

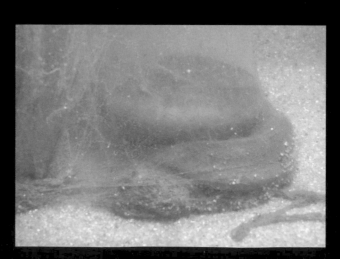

How much slime?

In just minutes, an adult hagfish can secrete enough slime to turn a large bucket of water into gel. The gel has the consistency of wallpaper paste. This can clog up the mouth, eyes, throat, or gills of an attacker and suffocate it to death.

Spectacular, stretchy slime

Hundreds of glands lie along the hagfish's body. They produce an amazing amount of slime, which contains fine fibers that allow it to stretch without breaking.

Slime

Oozing

Barbels that detect dead flesh

Mouth without jaws

Gill openings for breathing

That's disgusting!

The hagfish has revolting feeding habits: it enters dead or dying sea creatures and eats them from the inside out. It ties itself into a knot to lever itself against the dead body—by doing so it pulls off chunks of flesh to eat.

Cleaning up

To clean the slime off, I tie myself into a knot, running it down my body so that it wipes off the slime.

Pulling the trigger!

Size comparison

The colorful family of fish known as triggerfish is common on coral reefs. Triggerfish have flat bodies and swiveling eyes set high on their heads. Their name comes from a "trigger" mechanism that controls their defensive spines.

Locked spine
The large dorsal spine is locked in an upright position.

Spine Mechanism

1   2   3

When the large dorsal spine is raised, a smaller spine (the "trigger") lifts up to lock it in an upright position (figure 1). If the "trigger" is pressed down, it releases the big spine (figure 2). Both spines fold down neatly (figure 3).

Bolt-hole
A triggerfish heads for a safe crack. The fish's slim body slips easily into narrow spaces.

Strong jaws
The jaws of a triggerfish are extremely powerful for their size.

Tough covering
For extra protection, triggerfish have very tough body scales, like armor plating.

To escape from predators, a triggerfish hides in a rock or coral crevice and erects a spiny fin on its back. This triggers another spine, which springs up to lock the first one in position. The spines wedge the fish tightly in its hole and nothing can dislodge it. When the fish feels safe again, it lowers the spines to release itself.

Confused clown?
The fantastic clown triggerfish can't seem to decide which pattern it likes best.

Huff and puff
A blue triggerfish attacks a spiny sea urchin by blowing out jets of water to bowl it over.

Crunch!
A moustache triggerfish cracks through a thick shell to reach the tasty treat inside.

DO NOT
ENTER

THE CONE ZONE

Triggerfish fiercely protect their nesting territory, which covers a cone-shaped zone (see picture), with the point of the cone starting at the nest. A diver who swims upward to escape an angry fish stays in the danger area, and may get chased. Swimming SIDEWAYS is the best way out of trouble.

TEETH made for BITING

Scuba divers often meet triggerfish around the reefs. It's not the spines that divers need to worry about, but the TEETH. Triggerfish have small mouths but they have extremely strong teeth. These fish feed on things with hard, crunchy shells, like sea urchins, clams, oysters, and snails. So they have no problem biting through a wetsuit if a diver annoys them. Some divers have come to the surface with triggerfish teeth marks in their ears, fingers, and feet!

Synchronized Swimming

STICKING TOGETHER

Most fish love company. Many swim around in large groups called schools like these chevron barracuda and bigeye jacks in the Pacific Ocean. There's safety in numbers, and more than 200 pairs of eyes are better than one when it comes to spotting a predator.

APPLE OF HIS EYE

THE HUMPBACK
WHALE is a huge creature
that can reach 50 ft (15 m)
in length, yet it's an agile
swimmer. It has a large head
and an exceptionally long
jaw in relation to the size
of its body.

Despite this whale's immense size,
each of its eyeballs is only about
the size of an apple.

Animals at risk—

Many marine species are **threatened,** on a scale from VULNERABLE through endangered to EXTINCT.

NAME: Marine iguana
Amblyrhynchus cristatus
STATUS: vulnerable
The only sea-going lizard, the marine iguana lives on the Galápagos Islands, where it faces predation by cats and dogs brought to the islands by settlers.

NAME: Atlantic cod
Gadus morhua
STATUS: vulnerable
Its popularity as a fish dinner has led to the decline of the once plentiful Atlantic cod. Several stocks collapsed in the 1990s through overfishing and they have not recovered.

NAME: Great white shark
Carcharodon carcharias
STATUS: vulnerable
Despite being the scariest fish in the ocean, this widely feared top predator is not as invincible as you might think. Although it is not hunted for food, its fearsome reputation makes it a target for some game fishermen and commercial hunters, who capture it for its teeth, jaws, and fins.

NAME: Blue whale
Balaenoptera musculus
STATUS: endangered
The biggest animal on the planet, the blue whale was almost hunted to extinction in the first half of the 20th century. Since the 1960s it has been protected, but there are still fewer than an estimated 5,000 left.

NAME: Tucuxi
Sotalia fluviatilis
STATUS: data unknown
Found in coastal waters and estuaries around northern South America, these small dolphins are at increasing risk from fishing nets, tourist boats, and river pollution.

who's on the missing list?

The causes include **habitat loss**, pollution, *harvesting*, and being **eaten** by introduced species—which can all be traced back to PEOPLE.

NAME: Common seahorse
Hippocampus kuda
STATUS: vulnerable
Less common than its name suggests, this species is suffering from over-collection for the aquarium industry and use in traditional medicines.

NAME: Coelacanth
Latimeria chalumnae
STATUS: critically endangered
Once believed to be extinct, the identification of a specimen caught off the Comoros Islands in 1938 led to a hunt for this "living fossil." Since then, several hundred have been caught. Another species has been found living near Sulawesi, Indonesia.

NAME: Sea otter
Enhydra lutris
STATUS: endangered
Sea otters are an important keystone species in their ecosystem. They eat sea urchins that would otherwise devour the kelp forests that act as homes and food to other species.

NAME: Hawksbill turtle
Eretmochelys imbricata
STATUS: critically endangered
Their long lifespan and slow reproductive rates make sea turtles particularly vulnerable. This species is hunted for its meat and decorative shell.

NAME: Rainbow parrotfish
Scarus guacamaia
STATUS: vulnerable
Destruction of its mangrove nursery habitat has left this beaked reef-dweller with fewer safe havens for its young. Other threats include pollution, overfishing, and coastal development.

HAVE WE SEEN THE LAST OF THEM?

69

Talking Fish

Who said that?

Fish may not chat over a cup of coffee, but they do make noises to communicate. Using a wide variety of sounds, they tell each other where to find food, warn off strangers, look for a mate, and check which creatures are friends and which are foes.

Chirp, chirp.
Chirp, chirp.

The croaker and the spotted drum both belong to a family of fish known for making loud "drumming" noises as a sign that they are ready to mate. Like the damselfish, these creatures produce their characteristic sound by vibrating their swim bladders.

Some species of **triggerfish** make a sound similar to a "grunt" or a "snarl" when they are threatened.

Male damselfish are highly territorial. When they're chasing away intruders (or rivals for a mate), they produce "chirping" and "popping" sounds. When they're trying to attract a female, they just chirp. Females also chirp and pop when they feel threatened. Both sexes produce these sounds by using special muscles to vibrate their swim bladders (an internal pocket of air that helps the fish maintain its balance).

SNARL

Pop, pop.

70

Grunts

"grunt" by rubbing two of their back teeth together. In this fish, the swim bladder acts as a resonating chamber, helping to make the sound louder.

Z

Z

Boom Boom

Grunt

Z

Oyster toadfish males

attract females with a loud "booming" sound (like a boat foghorn), again made by vibrating the walls of their swim bladders. Some people compare the noise to the sound of a passing subway train!

Z

Click, click!

Seahorses and pipefish "snap" and "click" as part of their courtship ritual. These sounds are made when the edges of two bones on the top of the skull rub together.

Gobies
also make sounds during courtship, as well as slightly pulsing "snore" noises when intruders approach their territory.

Herring make high-pitched "farting"
noises by expelling air from their swim bladders out their anuses (kind of like using the swim bladder as a whoopee cushion). Herring are only really noisy after dark, so they may produce this sound to help them find each other when they can't see very well.

Excuse me!

CHANGING

An Australian giant cuttlefish measuring nearly 5 ft (1.5 m) hovers in shallow water in the breeding season. He is putting on an impressive color-changing display to attract a female.

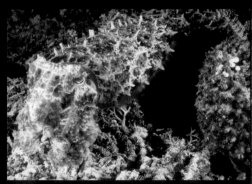

Cuttlefish have special pigment cells under their skin that can change color instantly and produce a mesmerizing display. In males, vivid stripes of colors pulse over their bodies as they compete for a mate.

1 A cuttlefish matches its background perfectly.

2 Now it is beginning to change its color...

3 ... and its outline starts to become clearer...

COLORS

swim companionably beside each other, the tentacles of one seeming to "stroke" the other. In fact, the outer tentacles of the cuttlefish conceal a killer pair hidden inside. These can elongate suddenly to snatch an unsuspecting fish or crab and stuff it into the cuttlefish's mouth.

Cuttlefish have good eyesight, with binocular vision, and use this to find their prey. Like their relatives, octopuses and squid, they can squirt a cloud of black ink through their siphon to confuse attackers, allowing them time to escape.

Cuttlefish don't only change color to attract females, they also change color to...

... camouflage themselves.

... show mood.

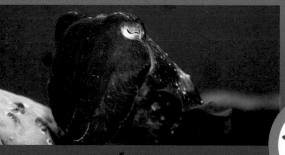

... confuse prey.

4 ... and clearer...

5 ... and clearer.

6 The change happens in a matter of seconds.

RECORD BREAKERS

SPEEDY SWIMMERS

Both the **killer whale** (*Orcinus orca*) and **Dall's porpoise** (*Phocoenoides dalli*) have been recorded swimming at speeds of around 35 mph (56 kph). They are the world's fastest mammals in the ocean! The killer whale also holds the title for the largest species of the oceanic dolphin family. It's a real record breaker!

deepest smallest loudest fastest longest biggest deepest

Fastest FISH

Cosmopolitan sailfish This is the world's fastest fish over short distances—it has been tested to have a top speed of 68 mph (110 kph). By contrast, the cheetah's top speed is around 62 mph (100 kph).

Biggest JELLYFISH

Lion's mane jellyfish Found in the chilly waters of the North Atlantic and North Pacific and around the coasts of northern Europe, specimens have been measured that were nearly 8 ft (2.5 m) across the bell, with tentacles up to 120 ft (37 m) long.

Largest INVERTEBRATE

Colossal squid Most squid are under 2 ft (60 cm) long, and giant squid may reach 43 ft (13 m). But an even bigger species was found in 2003—colossal squid (*Mesonychoteuthis hamiltoni*), which may grow to 46 ft (14 m), making it the largest invertebrate in existence.

A blue whale can dive as far down as 655 ft (200 m). It raises its tail in the air and then uses its powerful back muscles to propel itself into the depths.

Biggest CRUSTACEAN

Giant spider crab This crab lives on the bottom of the Pacific Ocean around Japan. Its normal leg span is about 8–9 ft (2.5–2.75 m)—the largest on record spanned almost 13 ft (4 m) and weighed nearly 42 lb (19 kg).

LONGEST-LIVING FISH

Rougheye rockfish It's hard to work out how long fish live in the wild—their ages can only be estimated by tagging, or counting growth rings in scales or earbones. Rougheye rockfish, found in the Pacific, are thought to live for up to 205 years.

Rougheye rockfish

loudest deepest

Most valuable FISH

Beluga sturgeon This sturgeon's eggs are cleaned, then dried or salted to turn them into caviar, one of the world's most expensive foods. One female, caught in 1924, yielded around 540 lb (245 kg) of top-quality caviar—worth over $1.5 million today!

Smallest FISH ⌄

Stout infantfish The smallest and lightest of marine fish—and shortest known vertebrate—lives in Australia's Great Barrier Reef. Only six have ever been found. Males are around ¼ in (7 mm)—females are slightly larger.

Most poisonous FISH

Maki maki One of the most poisonous fish in the world, Maki maki is found in the Red Sea and Indian Ocean. It produces a powerful poison in its liver.

Deepes DEPTH

The Mariana trench, in the Pacific Ocean off Japan, is about 7 miles (11 km) deep. It is the deepest area in all the world's oceans.

Largest MOLLUSK

Giant clam In 1965, an example was found that measured 56 in (137 cm) across. Another, found in 1917, measured 49 in (120 cm) across and weighed 580 lb (263 kg).

Farthest FLIGHT

Flying fish These don't actually fly; they glide over the water on specially enlarged and stiffened fins. Depending on wind and sea conditions, some can glide for over 660 ft (200 m), reaching heights of up to 33 ft (10 m).

LOUDES' ocean animal

Blue, fin, and bowhead whales The low-frequency-communication pulses emitted by blue whales, fin whales, and bowhead whales have been measured at 186–189 decibels, making them the loudest known sounds emitted by any living creature. In contrast, a jumbo jet taking off measures 120 decibels.

LONGEST worm

Bootlace worm This is the longest sea worm, and probably the longest of all worms. It lives in the shallow waters of the North Sea. One specimen washed ashore in 1864 measured over 180 ft (55 m) long.

Biggest CREATURE

Blue whale Not only the biggest creature in the sea, this is also the biggest living animal in the world. In 1926, a blue whale measuring 110 ft (33.6 m) long (as large as a jet plane) was captured in the Shetland Islands, off Scotland. Its heart was the size of a small car, and its tongue had a big enough area for 50 people to stand on.

LONGEST-LIVING CREATURE

Ocean quahog One of these clams was plucked from water 260 ft (80 m) deep off the north coast of Iceland in 2007. After examination, scientists estimated it was between 405 and 410 years old. (This may be the longest-living animal ever!)

Ocean quahog

HIGH SEAS drifters

Going with the flow
The name plankton comes from the Greek word for "drifter." And that's exactly what plankton does—travel on the oceans' currents.

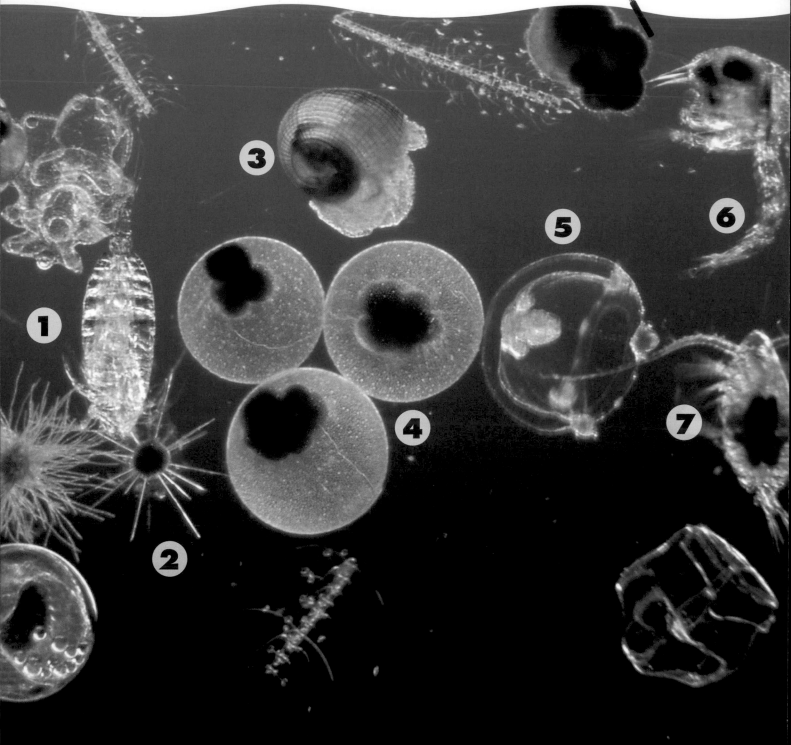

Life in the sunlit zone is very crowded. Although you cannot **see** them, the surface waters of our oceans are teeming with **billions of trillions** of microscopic animals, plants, and bacteria called **plankton**. They spend all their lives drifting with the tide.

1. Sea cucumber larva **2.** Radiolarian **3.** Snail larva **4.** Fish eggs **5.** Jellyfish **6.** Shrimp larva **7.** Copepod

Phytoplankton

Phytoplankton are minute plants that live near the ocean's surface. Sunlight is essential for photosynthesis, which provides the plant with energy. They also take nutrients out of the water to help them grow. The main types are diatoms, dinoflagellates, and blue-green algae.

Zooplankton

Zooplankton are tiny animals. They range in size from jellyfish down to microscopic forms that are just one cell. Zooplankton can be split into two groups. Holoplankton spend their whole lives as zooplankton and include krill and copepods. Meroplankton consist of the eggs and larvae of fish, crustaceans, and other marine animals that will eventually grow into free-swimming or bottom-dwelling organisms.

Bacterioplankton

These microscopic organisms play an important part in the breakdown of organic material and the recycling of minerals.

If chalk could talk
It's hard to imagine, but these tall cliffs are made from the bodies of dead plankton. Limestone and chalk are rocks made from the tiny skeletons of plants and animals. When they die, the skeletons sink to the seafloor. Millions of years and trillions of tons of dead plankton later, you have a cliff.

Bloomin' amazing
When there are lots of nutrients in the water the number of phytoplankton can increase dramatically. These algal blooms, as they are called, can even be seen from space. This one happened off the west coast of Ireland. The pale blue area in the middle of the picture is the bloom.

Phytoplankton

Zooplankton

Herring

Sea lion

Killer whale

Chain gang
Plankton are the start of the marine food chain. Phytoplankton and bacterioplankton take nutrients from the water so they can grow. Both are eaten by zooplankton, which become food for small fish and squid. These are then eaten by bigger and bigger animals all the way up to killer whales and great white sharks.

GLOSSARY

Abyssal zone the area of the ocean that reaches depths of 13,000–20,000 ft (4,000–6,000 m).

Algae simple plants that include seaweeds and phytoplankton.

Amino acids chemical compounds that are used to make proteins.

Anadromous fish marine-living fish that return to their freshwater birthplace to spawn.

Baleen the tough, flexible, comblike plates that some whales use to filter plankton out of water. Also known as whalebone.

Barb a backward-facing point on a spine or stinger that lodges into flesh, preventing it from being pulled back out. Also the name of a family of fish.

Bioluminescence a chemical reaction by which an animal produces light.

Camouflage patterns or colors that help an animal blend in with its background and hide from enemies.

Cartilage a tough and flexible structural material that forms a shark's skeleton.

Cnidarian a member of a group of animals that have stinging cells called nematocysts. Jellyfish and corals are cnidarians.

Crustacean animal that has a jointed, segmented body and a hard shell. Crabs, shrimp, and lobsters are crustaceans.

Digestive system the parts of the body that break down food so that it can be absorbed.

Echinoderm a group of animals that have tube feet, a five-rayed symmetry, and no head. Starfish and sea urchins are echinoderms.

Estuary the area where a river meets the ocean.

Exoskeleton the outer skeleton of a crustacean.

Extinction the point at which the last animal or plant of a species ceases to exist in the wild.

Gills the delicate feathery structures through which animals breathe under water. Gills absorb oxygen from the water and release waste carbon dioxide back into it.

Hadal zone an area of extremely deep water that lies below the abyssal zone, usually where the seabed drops to form a trench.

Invertebrate an animal without a backbone. All crustaceans are invertebrates, as are marine worms, snails, sea slugs, corals, starfish, and sea cucumbers.

Iridescence an optical effect in which something appears to change color when viewed from a different angle. Fish scales often display iridescent colors.

Krill a tiny, shrimplike animal found in all oceans. They are a major source of food for many animals, including blue whales.

Mammal an animal that has hair or fur and feeds its young on milk. Seals and dolphins are mammals.

Mollusk a member of a group of soft-bodied animals that are either shell-less or have only a thin shell. Octopuses, snails, clams, and squid are all types of mollusk.

Nutrients the essential chemicals that an organism feeds on.

Parasite a small organism that lives on or inside the body of a bigger organism, feeding on it at the host's expense.

Pelagic zone any area of open ocean that is not close to the seabed. Creatures that swim in it are described as pelagic.

Photophores the light-producing organs found on many deep-water animals that make them bioluminescent.

Photosynthesis the process by which plants and algae use sunlight to make food.

Pigment this is a chemical compound that gives something its color.

Plankton microscopic plants and animals that drift in the water, providing a supply of food for other animals. Divided into phytoplankton (plants) and zooplankton (animals).

Predator an animal that kills and eats other animals.

Prey an animal that is killed and eaten by a predator is called prey.

Rorqual the name given to the largest group of baleen whales, which includes the blue, humpback, and Minke whales.

Spawning the production or deposition of large amounts of eggs into water so that they can be fertilized with sperm and develop into young animals.

Species a type of organism. The members of a species can breed with each other to produce fertile offspring.

Sperm the male reproductive cells that fertilize a female's eggs to create new animals.

Submersible a small underwater exploratory craft.

Swim bladder the organ in bony fish that helps them stay at the same position in the water without needing to use their fins.

Tentacles long, flexible structures found around the mouth of many creatures. They are used for sensing, grasping, or feeding.

Territory the area in which an animal lives and hunts and which it will defend against intruders.

Venom a poisonous substance in an animal's bite or sting.

Vertebrate an animal that has a backbone. Fish, whales, and seals are all vertebrates.

Giant Pacific octopus
(*Enteroctopus dofleini*)

INDEX

algae 45, 77
anadromy 34–35
angel fish 37
anglerfish 21, 45, 46
arthropods 9
barnacle 26
barracuda 37
batfish
    rosy-lipped 25
bathyscaphe 20
bioluminescence 20, 44–45, 47
black-spotted sweetlip fish 37
blobfish 25
blubber 29
blue-striped dwarf goby 10
blue-striped grunt fish 42
breathing 10, 32, 58–59
brittle stars 9
catfish 38
chordates 9
clams 9, 21, 30, 37
    giant 74
cleaning stations 42–43
clownfish 7, 37
cnidarians 8
cod 32, 68
copepods 21, 76
corals 7, 8, 26, 42–43, 51, 54, 62
crabs 9,
    hermit 26, 32
    kelp 6
crustaceans 45, 77
cuttlefish 9, 72–73
Dall's porpoise 74
damselfish 70
deep-sea cucumber 47
defenses 50
diving 20–21
dogfish 10, 15
    spiny 15
dolphins 6, 9, 13, 20
dugongs 12
eating 18–19, 61
echinoderms 9
echolocation 13
eels
    electric 38
    gulper 24
    moray 43
    ribbon 25
electric fish 38–39
emperor angel fish 27
endangered species 68–69
fangtooth 47
fish 10–11, 32–33
fish louse 27
flatfish 21
flounder, peacock 22–23
frogfish 25
giant spider crab 74
gilded pipefish 37
goby 71
goldfish 32
grouper 43
grunts 71
hagfish 25, 60–61
hatchet fish 47
herrings 6, 9, 71, 77
invertebrates 8–9
isopods 21
jellyfish 8, 20, 21, 37, 45, 50, 52–53, 74, 77
krill 7, 18, 19
lionfish 37
lobsters 9

maki maki 75
mammals 12–13
manatees 12
Mariana trench 75
marine iguana 68
marine otters 6
marlin 6
microbes 77
mollusks 9, 30
mussels 30
nautilus 31
ocean quahog 75
ocean zones 6, 20–21, 46–47,
octopuses 7, 9, 20, 51
orange-spotted shrimp goby 37
oysters 9
oyster toadfish 71
parrotfish 54–55, 69
penguins 7
plankton 76
    phytoplankton 20–21, 77
    zooplankton 77
porcupine fish 56
porpoises 13
Portuguese man-o-war 52–53
radiolarian 76
ragworm 27
rays 9, 32
    stingrays 51
    torpedo 38
rockfish
    blue rockfish 6
    rougheye 74
rorquals 19
sailfish, cosmopolitan 74
salmon 9, 26, 34–35
sardines 6
scallops 9, 30
scorpionfish 24
sea anemones 7, 8
sea cucumbers 7, 9, 20, 76
sea dragon 27
sea grass 27
seahorses 69, 71
sea lilies 37
sea lions 12, 35, 77
seals 9, 12
sea otters 6, 69
sea slugs 9
sea snails 9
sea snakes 9, 51
sea spiders 9
    giant sea spider 74
sea trout 37
sea urchins 6, 9, 31, 50
seaweeds 6
    kelp 6
sharks 6, 7, 9, 14–15, 16–17, 20, 32, 50
    blacktip reef 15
    bull 15
    great white 32, 50, 68
    hammerhead 14
    shortfin mako 14
    whale 10
shells 30
shrimp 9, 35, 43
slime eel see hagfish
snails
    larva 76
    turban snails 6
spawning 34–35
spines 31, 51, 56
sponges 8
spotted drum 70

squid 9, 20, 35, 44, 45
    colossal 74
    giant 74
starfish 7, 9, 20
    crown of thorns 51
stargazer 38
stone fish 51
stout infantfish 10, 75
sturgeon, beluga 75
submersibles 20
swimming 11, 12, 32, 64
triggerfish 62–63, 70
tube worms 20
tucuxi 68
tuna 6
turtles, 20, 37, 69
vertebrates 8–9
viperfish 24, 47
walruses 7, 9, 12
whales 9, 12, 13, 18–19, 26, 28–29, 58–59
    baleen 18, 28
    blowholes 58–59
    blue 19, 68, 74, 75
    bowhead 19, 75
    fin 19, 75
    gray 19
    humpback 66–67
    killer (orca) 35, 74, 77
    Minke 19
    right 19
    sperm 20, 28
worms 8
    bootlace 75
    bristle worms 8
    flatworms 8
    tube worms 8
wrasse 43

Caribbean reef shark
(*Carcharhinus perezi*)

Yellowtail snapper
(*Ocyurus chrysurus*)

Scuba diver

CREDITS

Dorling Kindersley would like to thank Devika Dwarkadas, Parul Gambhir, Aradhana Gupta, and Vaibhav Rastogi for design assistance.